BLUFF YOUR WAY IN
WHISKY

DAVID MILSTED

RAVETTE BOOKS

Published by Ravette Books Limited
Egmont House
8 Clifford Street
London W1X 1RB
(071) 734 0221

First printed 1991
Reprinted 1992, 1993

Series Editor – Anne Tauté

Cover design – Jim Wire
Printing & Binding – Cox & Wyman Ltd.
Production – Oval Projects Ltd.

CONTENTS

CONTENTS (Continued)

INTRODUCTION

The wonderful thing about whisky, apart of course, from drinking it, is that it contains more bluffing elements than almost any other subject – far more than supply-side economics, more even than wine. Wine breeds envy, discord and snobbery, whisky promotes fellowship, amiability and quiet, unassuming superiority. Supply-side economics produced Donald Trump.

Until quite recently whisky was a subject that tended to be monopolised by Scots, foreigners, and elderly gentlemen in Clubs. This made the whole area fairly barren ground for bluffers unless they were fortunate enough to find themselves in the company of North Americans with remote Highland ancestry. Such people have a pleasing habit of believing pretty well anything, up to and including the social benefits of the clan system and the romantic joys of kelp-gathering.

Things have changed. Whisky appreciation is an idea whose time has come. It will bring you into contact with much nicer people. Real people. Caring people… People like us.

Like all the best things in life, whisky is a fairly simple business that can easily be made to sound exclusive and impressive by a judicious application of the arcane and a liberal sprinkling of jargon. Knowledge of whisky, like love, is a matter of a basic theme made more enjoyable by an infinite number of variations. The really experienced may even find themselves able to combine the two, a thing real ale enthusiasts could never do.

Unlike that other great source of pleasure, however, whisky offers a field of activity in which a rapid turnover of partners (there are approximately 1,182 Scottish ones currently available) is positively beneficial. When in doubt, play safe – pour another dram.

Whisky is a subject steeped in mystery and tradition. Since most of this is completely unknown to the average whisky drinker, the amount of hard work required on your part is reassuringly small. There are two eternal truths about whisky:

1. No two whiskies are alike
2. 99 per cent of whisky drinkers can't tell the difference until it's revealed to them.

Keep pointing out number (1) while bearing number (2) in mind, and you can't go wrong.

———————

'If a body could just find out the exact proper proportion and quantity that ought to be drunk every day, and keep to that, I verily trow that he might live forever…and that doctors and kirkyards would go out of fashion.'

James Hogg

'Malt does more than Milton can
To justify God's ways to man.'   **Historic whisky ad**

'When I drink, I think: and when I think, I drink.'

François Rabelais

'There are two things best taken naked, and one of them is whisky.'   **Gaelic proverb**

WHAT IS WHISKY?

The dictionary defines whisky as:

(1) *Spirit distilled from malted barley, other grains, or potatoes, etc.*

(2) *Kind of light gig or chaise.*

which is precise, lucid, incontrovertible, and most unhelpful unless you happen to be a romantic historical novelist. This is ideal for whisky-bluffers, of course, because it gives you practically unlimited scope for improvisation.

'Whisky' – which used to be called 'whisky-bar' – is derived from the Gaelic *uisge beatha* (pronounced 'ooshki baah') meaning 'water of life'. The ancient Romans called their alcohol *aqua vitae*, which sounds remarkably similar, if you make the effort.

The noble and ancient human art of distilling is known to have been practised in Asia around 800 BC and is believed to have been introduced by St. Patrick to Ireland from Scotland (*not* the other way round) before being re-exported by St. Columba.

The avatar of all whiskies is **Ferintosh**, an incredibly ancient, semi-apocryphal liquor, drunk by Methusela to celebrate his 900th. 'The real Ferintosh' is thus the ultimate accolade but should only be applied to something you drank once, long ago. It was last made, duty-free, by the Forbes family of Culloden; the ending of this civilised arrangement towards the close of the eighteenth century caused Robert Burns (a former exciseman) to write:

'O Ferintosh, o sadly lost!'

Like much of Burns' best poetry, this sounds better if you've had a whisky or two.

Varieties

There are four of these to get to grips with, *viz:* **Malt whisky, Grain whisky, Blended whisky**, and **Others**.

(1) Malt Whisky

Malt whisky should always be called **malt** and thought of as the Real Stuff. Successful malt-bluffing involves the only remotely hard work you have to do, which is to memorise a few key words to describe the important elements of the process distillers go through to make it. These are set out in ravishing detail later on (see **Glossary – The Process**); meanwhile, all you need to remember is that it's made entirely from barley, using a **pot-still**. This is important.

Malt whisky distilling is a beautifully simple process, and anyone with a reasonably large, plumbed-in potting shed could do it – if it weren't for spoilsports like Customs and Excise whose job it is to ensure that the simple, wholesome pleasures of life cost 75 per cent more per bottle than they ought to.

(2) Grain Whisky

Grain whisky is made from maize (as are cornflakes) which is ground up and mixed with a little malted barley (usually in a ratio of 9:1). Fermentation then takes place before distillation in a **patent still** (or **Coffey still**, named after the cunning profiteer who invented it) to emerge as **silent spirit** – an alcoholic substance that may as easily be used for making gin or vodka, as Scotch whisky.

You can be very rude about the patent still; compare

it unfavourably with a petro-chemical works or a bunch of plastic daffodils. A patent still is to a pot-still what a Trechikoff is to a Rubens.

Deplore it even as you consume its product in the form of:

(3) Blended Whisky

A mixture of malt and grain, of which more later.

(4) Other Whiskies

These are what the dictionary editors had in mind when they wrote 'etc'.

Irish Whiskey

Irish whiskey is made in much the same way as Scottish malt whisky, except that it's distilled three times instead of two. This makes it smoother and rounder (or, if you prefer, blander) than Scottish malt, and presumably accounts for the higher price per bottle.

Irish whiskey tastes sweeter because no peat is used to kiln the malt; this is odd for a country that has more bog per hectare than anywhere else on the planet (probably) and possibly has something to do with the fact that 98.4 per cent of Irish peat ends up in garden centres.

Point out that Irish whiskey is spelled differently from Scotch whisky because the ancient Scots (who were originally Irish) spoke a different sort of Gaelic to the ancient Irish (who were originally Hungarian). In fact, Scotch whisky was also spelled with an 'e' up to around the time of the 1916 Easter Rebellion.

Irish whiskey can also be made with potatoes and

called *poteen*. This is (a) illegal, and (b) not highly recommended.

Bourbon

A North American whisky made from maize and rye in an attempt to compensate for the lack of bens, glens, bogs, midges, rain and lost causes, so essential to the making of the Real Stuff. Named after Aristophanes Q. Bourbon III, famous Kentucky inventor of the chocolate sandwich biscuit.

Sour Mash

Another trans-Atlantic ex-colonial imitation, so called because of the addition of acetic acid to the cereal grains in order to chivvy along the fermentation process. Also known as **sippin' whisky**, presumably because only an idiot would risk taking a whole mouthful. It may be that idiots are especially thick on the ground in Tennessee, but it is probably wiser not to speculate.

Japanese Whisky

According to a Scots distiller 'If you drank it all day and all night you might end up thinking it was like Scotch whisky. But by then you might be dead.'

Japan's efforts to make the water of life range from importing bulk malt whisky and mixing it with neutral spirit, to producing an instant powdered whisky (just add instant soda). On the other hand, Suntory Japanese whisky is the world's leading brand, and has a 30 per cent stake in Islay's Bowmore distillery. This is a sobering thought – enough to make you rush out and buy a case or two of the Real Stuff.

Liqueur Whisky

There is considerable debate as to whether 'liqueur whiskies' like *Drambuie* and *Glayva* ought to be regarded as whiskies at all, and we suggest you prolong discussions until the bottle in question has been squeezed dry. In favour of classing them as whiskies is the fact that they all have varying amounts of whisky in them, but then, so does whisky-mac (a mixture of whisky and ginger wine). On the other hand they all contain unforgivable things like herbs, honey, and fruit and ought therefore to belong firmly in the 'sticky' class, along with those dark chocolates with the centres that taste of expensive cough linctus. It can be a fascinating post-prandial debate, particulary if someone else is buying.

Note that 'Drambuie' derives from the Gaelic for 'yellow drink', and feel free to speculate whether it would have been half so successful if it had been sold under this name. Dismiss any suggestion that it derives from *an dram buidheach* – 'the drink that satisfies' – as a mere marketing ploy. Scotland is full of hills called Ben Buie and lochs called Loch Buie, and none of them is supposed to be satisfying.

The secret recipe for *Drambuie* was supposed to have been given to a Captain MacKinnon of Skye by Charles Edward Stuart as a thankyou for not betraying him to the English. Bonnie Prince Charlie then went to Rome and drank himself to death – not, you should hasten to add, on whisky.

MALT WHISKY

As well as being, on its own, the noblest drink on earth, malt whisky also finds its way (albeit sometimes in minute quantities) into every bottle of blended Scotch whisky, however cheap and cheerful; without it, Britain's laughably misnamed Balance of Payments would look a whole lot worse. Yet it is the product of only a hundred-odd working distilleries north of Hadrian's Wall.

Malt accounts for a substantial portion of the lore, mystique and hagiography (not to mention the bunkum and balderdash) of whisky, and your pretence to a good grounding in its various **elements, types** and **regions** will thus form an essential part of any successful attempt to beguile, hoodwink, hoax, humbug or otherwise hornswoggle innocent bystanders in your vicinity.

The Bluffing Elements

All that kilning, malting, brewing, distilling and casking (see **Glossary**) provides a wealth of material for the meretriciously educated bluffer.

Begin with just one element of this process and, when you've proved your ability, proceed to two or more in combination – but take care not to end up contradicting yourself by (for example) demonstrating that the water used to distil your whisky makes it ethereally pure and fragrant while at the same time maintaining that the peat used to malt the barley contributes to its sooty pungency. Your best plan, should you see such a blatant self-contradiction looming, is to proclaim it a 'manifest synthesis'.

12

Picture yourself dram in hand and eager to say something memorable about it. *Ah,* you begin, *now what we have here is very interesting, you see, because of . . .*

Water

One of the principal variables of whisky, water should enable you to anatomise the contents of your glass in terms that leave the average wine enthusiast eating your dust.

Water is one of the reasons why Scotch whisky cannot be made outside Scotland, the assumption being that Scottish water is pure and clean, and *soft* – the sort of water that foams if you wave a bar of soap over it. This is most true of the Highlands, which aren't blighted by factories, chemical waste dumps, junk bond dealers and so forth.

Enthuse about its unique 'Highland qualities', that is to say extremely wet, and ready-infused with mystic trace elements of peat, granite, heather, midge, tweed, damp, and Roman Ninth Legion. Its origin is as important in the production of **Speyside malts** (see **Regions**), for instance, as hard Trent water is in the brewing of Burton Ale, and it can't be imitated.

Refer to variables of:

• **Supply**
  Does it come from a spring, a burn, a river, or a loch? Is it the crystal-clear stuff contained in bottles or the high-fibre variety that stains enamel baths brown in Ardnamurchan?

13

- **Season**

  The biochemical profile of Scottish water may be completely altered by a period of heavy rain or (slightly less common) a heatwave. This can cause wide variation between two batches of whisky from the same distillery; it is therefore the main source of impressive-sounding hogwash for the **single-cask malt**, and the rough equivalent of a wine-bore's 'late vintage' ploy.

Tell the story of two single malt whiskies *Glen Mhor* and *Glen Albyn* – the produce of two distilleries situated a few hundred yards apart on the banks of the River Ness. Both, according to reliable authority, use the same malt, peat, yeast, size and type of still and cask: each is matured for the same period. Yet the difference in taste between the two is unmistakable. The only thing that could possibly account for this is the water: each draws its supply from a different source in the river. This, at any rate, was the story of their late proprietor, and if he was prepared to stick to it, we can too.

Barley

Most distillers will insist that the source and type of their barley has no influence on the taste or quality of their product; this is because most distillers these days have very little control over where their barley comes from, or what sort it is. Where once Scotland's distilleries were self-sufficient in grain, often grown in their own fields, now it might as easily come from Ireland, England, Canada, the United States or even Australia. Point out that origin and type of grain is a significant and variable factor.

If you dislike your dram, try saying: 'I fear this has been made with barley from . . .' [insert a nation from the list above]. Then drink it anyway, just to be sociable.

If your drink tastes 'bready', blame over-enthusiasm in the grinding mill; if you find it tends to cauterize your nostrils before your lips can get to it, make a passing reference to 'original moisture', the moisture content of the barley after it's been malted; this is usually around 3 per cent but can be lower, as in whiskies that make you thirsty. It is another thing that distilleries who buy their grain ready-malted cannot properly control.

Alternatively mutter something about being able to detect a hint of decayed mouse droppings and suggest that the barley could not have been 'properly dressed'. With a bit of luck you may be allowed the rest of the bottle all to yourself.

Peat

Traditional distilleries kiln their malt over a peat furnace; modern ones puff peat smoke through it after kilning. Either way, peat is a crucial element. (Never call Irish whiskey 'peaty', remember, because the Irish don't use it.)

The splendid thing about peat is that it's very variable. Peat is formed from compressed layers of dead vegetation, so it takes its 'character' – chemical composition, mass, texture, aroma when burnt and so forth – from the nature of its changing environment, from prehistoric times right up to the day it was cut. Peat cut near the surface is porous, spongy, pale and rooty; the deeper you go, the denser and darker and more ancient it gets.

All this ought to give you plenty of scope for suggesting that the particular and unmistakable flavour/texture/afterburn of what you're drinking can be accounted for by the sheep droppings/seaweed/bog oak/giant elk/neolithic remains contained in the peat used in its manufacture. 'A hint of iodine on the tongue' you will pronounce 'is the unmistakable sign of a coastal distillery' (say Islay, Orkney or Caithness to be on the safe side). All you have to do is invent the evidence to match your conclusion.

As a general rule, you should insist that only malt whisky from a distillery that still cuts its own peat to kiln its own malt can count as the Real Stuff. But take care – you may find yourself championing one that cuts its peat on a site of special scientific interest inhabited by the Lesser Spotted Bog-Flopper and defended by hordes of environmentally-conscious television personalities.

If you need a clincher for your peat-bluff, observe that peat smoke contains **organic ring compounds with double carbon-carbon bonds** – a sure-fire sign of **pungency**. Few things are more effective than a strategically-deployed scientific fact.

Yeast

'Ah,' you murmur as you take another life-enhancing slurp of your host's supply, 'the perfect **zymurgy**' which is what happens when you ferment things – such as wort, in a distillery – with yeast.

Yeast is a living organism (whether it's an animal or not is the subject of heated debates among vegans) and it feeds on sugar to produce alcohol, a product which eventually kills it. Some yeasts are bred to produce greater quantities of alcohol before they peg out; there's even a yeast that is supposed to enable you to brew your own 'whisky' without going through the process (illegal, unless you're registered with Customs and Excise) of distilling it. We've tried it, and it's awful.

What you need to impress upon others is that:

a) distilleries use more than one type of yeast, and

b) very often these carefully selected yeasts have been used once already, in brewing. A quick search through records at Companies House has revealed to you the relationship between (for instance) *McEwan's Export* and *Isle of Jura* malt, or *Guinness Extra Stout* and *Dewar's*.

Yeast, you will insist, makes an essential contribution to the distinctive quality of a whisky – quite what that is, is entirely up to you. We recommend frequent use of the phrase 'almost intangible' for this one.

Pot-stills

The malt still, known as a pot-still, is one of the glories of creation. Made of gleaming, burnished copper its voluptuous belly curves gracefully upwards in one poignant swoop of beaten metal and then declines, with consummate, breathtaking artistry in a thrilling swan's-neck dive before descending into the hidden mysteries of the condenser.

The important thing to remember about pot-stills is that no two are exactly alike, a fact that puts them firmly in the 'bluffing variants' category. Some are squat onion-shaped affairs, others are the traditional pear shape; still others look like inverted tulip glasses. And each has its own special way of condensing the compounds in whisky. There are 600-800 compounds and how they relate to each other and how they affect the flavour has never been established. The only way to find out, of course, is through a lifetime's dedicated hard sampling.

Call science to your aid by remarking that the composition (always copper) and surface configuration of a pot-still determine the manner in which the chemical reactions take place. It's for this reason that old stills are supposedly replaced with new ones which are an exact replica of the original: this will lead you to the Famous Dented Still Myth, which you may safely apply to any distillery you choose to mention and use to justify your choice of something expensive when it's someone else's turn to pay.

The Famous Dented Still Myth

Once upon a time, in a distillery in Scotland, a stillman had an unfortunate accident, the exact circumstances of which are not clear, but whose consequence was that the spirit still sustained a severe dent.

Breath was bated until the first produce of the violated still was sampled, but the whisky was as excellent as always, and over the succeeding decades the still continued to pour forth a spirit sustaining alike to body and soul. In fact so successful was the dented still and so distinctive its yielded essence, that when the time came for it to wear out and be replaced, an identical dent was deliberately rendered in the replacement. Thus was the consistency of the product assured and maintained.

All you have to do is to sneak a look at the label and then tell the story as an explanation of why this is your favourite single malt. Your audience is unlikely to make the pilgrimage to the distillery to find out if you're bluffing – and if they do, the odds are they will find that you're not.

An additional still-bluff concerns **pot ale** – the gungy stuff left behind after the first distillation. What happens in many stills that are fired from below (as opposed to being steam-heated) is that the gunge can get itself cooked onto the bottom of the still and give that particular run of spirit a charcoaly-treacly flavour. To prevent this, the still is fitted inside with a large, slow-motion whisk called a **rummager**.

'Ah,' you rumble, rolling the golden blood of Scotia around your mouth before letting it slip sensuously down your throat, 'this has all the hallmarks of being cut from an *imperfectly rummaged run*.' In order to explain this fully, of course, you will need to sample at least one more large dram.

Cask   (Bluffese for 'barrel'.)

All whisky must mature for a minimum of three years in casks (unlike wine, it does not benefit from being kept in a bottle) and all casks must be made of oak. Zealots are fond of calling them 'oaken', a word much favoured by manufacturers who also put 'auld' on the label.

The three-year period for Scotch whiskies was imposed after exhaustive surveys of the Scottish climate, which tends towards the cooler, damper end of the meteorological spectrum (especially in the Northern Isles). Faster-maturing whisky will thus be one of the compensations of the latter stages of the Greenhouse Effect.

Australian Bonded Grand Liqueur, a product of Wm Teacher & Sons at the beginning of the century, was sent in casks to Australia in the belief that (a) the long sea voyage would aid the maturing process, and (b) Australians were hardly likely to notice if it didn't. Australia got its own back some years later by exporting Rupert Murdoch and the Minogues.

Many distilleries, especially those owned by a mega-consortium, have no control over their supply of casks and no idea what sort they're going to get next. This can have a dramatic effect on the colour (to say nothing of the texture, bouquet or palate) of the branded product – and, of course, gives you an ideal opening for explaining why your dram of Ben Thingy is lighter/darker/oilier/rounder/sharper than the last one you had.

The metal keg, we're relieved to state, is an indignity yet to be perpetrated: the flavour of whisky depends partly on its reaction with the components of wood. These are cellulose, hemicellulose, lignin and a host of volatile oils, acids, sugars, steroids, tannins, pigments and inorganic compounds (they have never succeeded in counting them all) providing free rein for the imaginative, uninhibited bluffer, especially if he or she has had a couple.

About 2 per cent of the maturing whisky is lost by evaporation: this is known as the **angels' share** and is the cause of much deep breathing in bonded warehouses. Mr Gladstone generously altered excise duty on whisky to take account of this loss. Lloyd-George, on the other hand, raised whisky duty by 39 per cent in 1939, tried to nationalise the Scottish distilleries in 1915, closed down all the pot-stills in 1917 and doubled the duty in 1918. He was not only Welsh, but a Temperance man, and probably insanely jealous.

Colour

Whisky begins its life as a colourless spirit and gains its hue in one of four ways; you will of course claim to distinguish between them:

1. Through being matured in old oak casks previously used for the storage of sherry, particularly oloroso and fino. This is the traditional, time-honoured, craft-hallowed way, and is hardly done any more.
   Claim to be drinking sherrified whisky if you can tell from the resonantly amber-clear look and tell-tale vinous grace-notes on the palate, or if you happen to know it's *The Macallan*.
2. Through being matured in spit-new oak casks that have had their insides briefly set on fire. Little specks of charcoal in your glass are a dead giveaway for this method.
3. By smearing the casks with **pajarette**, a brownish treacly stuff made from evaporated grape juice. Insist that this makes the whisky brownish, treacly, etc.
4. By painting them with caramel. Caramel is known to induce cancer in Californian rats; on the other hand, whisky probably cures them. It's a risk worth taking, on the whole.

Not surprisingly, only the diminishing band of category (1) whiskies will own up to the method used, though 90 per cent of 'All About Scotch Whisky' leaflets would have us believe it's universal. You might try remarking that a little gravy browning in one's dram is nothing compared with all the food dyes and agrochemicals that go into the average bottle of *vin rouge*.

Alternatively, venture to recommend **white whisky**. Matured without benefit of sherry cask, pajarette or

21

caramel but otherwise indistinguishable from ordinary whisky, white whisky has never really caught on, despite being marketed at about a pound a bottle less. It is inadvisable to admit an affection for it for no other reason than that, like vodka, it can be swigged from a Perrier bottle without arousing suspicion.

The Payoff

Sooner or later, some know-it-all is going to interrupt you and announce that all this stuff about peat and water and yeast and copper bellies and oak is nothing more than tales devised by the distillers to prop up the mystique of their product and keep their prices high. Your bluff, in other words, will be called.

Here we suggest you use the sad (but encouraging) story of the Alko Company, of Finland.

The Alko Story

Alko is the name of the Finnish state-owned booze company that has spent much of the past decade trying to distil a 'Scotch whisky' of its own in an effort to make the 24-hour winter evenings more bearable. Senior bluff-proof bøffins have succeeded in isolating 400 chemical compounds (out of the 800 or so available) which contribute to the flavour; 44 of these turn out to be in the oak used for the casks.

Using pot-stills specially made to imitate Speyside's finest, and yeast imported from Scotland, they have at last succeeded in producing a few bottles of Bonnie Helsinki Special Reserve Scottish-Type Whisky Drink. Thousands of Finns have so far failed to overcome their reserve about its content and Lalli Nykänen, head of the project, is on record as preferring to drink 12-year-old *Glenlivet*.

The Alko story touches on all the **bluffing elements** of your subject, and you should tell it whenever the bluff (not to mention the guff) gets tough. It's a salutary reminder of what happens to people who don't take bluffers seriously.

Types of Malt

Malt whisky can be bought and bluffed over in three varieties; these are, in descending order of affordability:

(1) **Vatted malt**

Expensive. Usually comes with an ornate label rich in scrolls and curlicues. A bottle of vatted malt contains malt whiskies from two or more distilleries – as opposed to a single malt, which is the unique product of one. The malts used are, you may safely say, often selected out of a suspicion that they're not quite good enough to make it on their own – though of course you must add (before you get sued) that some vatted malts are 'very good indeed'. Some people say they're bland, characterless and off-puttingly syrupy in flavour, but that's just their opinion.

What's lacking in a bottle of this sort is very often more than compensated for by adjectival overload on the label, where such words as 'fine', 'Royal', 'reserve', 'extra special', 'old', and even 'auld' proliferate. Unfortunately, it is often quite hard to find the bit where they tell you it's a mixture. What you need to look for is the missing word – in this case, 'single' or 'unblended' – and the missing information: the name and address of the distillery. Don't be misled by the word 'pure' – you wouldn't really expect it to have industrial effluent in it, after all.

Note that the age on the label must by law apply to the *youngest* whisky in the mixture, so a bottle of 8-year-old vatted malt will contain whiskies that are, ooh, eight years and a fortnight old, at least.

(2) **Single malt**

Even more expensive. There are over a hundred single malt whiskies, of which no more than half a dozen or so are likely to be available at your local store unless your local store happens to be in St. James', or you live in Elgin (*q.v.*). These will probably be the ones you see heavily advertised.

Malts come in a bewildering variety of ages (8, 10, 12, 15, 20, 25 and even, though this is pushing it a bit, 50 years) and proof strengths (70°, 75°, 80° and 100°). To be on the safe side, claim to enjoy best a brand matured for 12 years and bottled at a proof strength of 80°: it's the sort professional zealots usually go for. Anything less than this, you maintain, is best kept for people like your daughter's latest boyfriend; anything more is suitable only for people who need to be impressed, such as your bank manager (but not our bank manager, who's a splendid chap with a bottle of Bell's *Islander* for visitors).

Pick a more-or-less unheard of name – *Old Pulteney, MacPhail's, Glen Scotia, Glenesk, Glenturret, Scapa, Caperdonich, Ben Nevis, Cragganmore* – and insist that it is the only one worth drinking. Explain why by lavish association of **peat**, **pot-stills** and **water**.

Alternatively, simply say, 'Oh, it has to be **a Glenlivet**' – but not **The Glenlivet** – 'for me, every time.' This will open up whole new bluffing vistas (see **Glenlivet**).

Another virtually impregnable pose is to announce that the only malt whisky you'd be prepared to spend your hard-won earnings on is one which comes from a distillery that carries out every single process – from barley-steeping to cooperage – on the premises, using time-honoured methods dating back to the misty, romantic days of the Industrial Revolution. There aren't many that do this; indeed, as many Islay distilleries do it as in the whole of the rest of Scotland. As there are (at present) around 120 distilleries in the rest of Scotland and seven in Islay, the chances are that your companion's choice of tipple will not be the *real* Real Stuff. You will, of course, then proceed to reveal why it isn't – drinking as many samples as you can get away with in order to illustrate your exegesis.

Keep this going until you've convinced your listener that single malt whisky is the *sine qua non* of the distiller's art. It isn't, however; this distinction belongs to...

(3) **Single-cask malt**

Utterly pocket-crippling. In real life, supplies of this spirit are only available to the likes of merchant bankers, ageing rock stars, senior government advisers, judges and advertising executives, diocesan bishops, chat-show hosts, emirs and excisemen – that is to say, all those who deserve it least – but that shouldn't prevent you pretending to have a secret source who is a thirty-third degree Freemason.

We can all dream.

Single malt is the produce of a single distillery – but of several distillations, blended together in an effort to ensure product consistency. The phrase 'ten-year-old malt' can cover up to twelve months' production from a number of stills. A **single-cask** malt, on the other hand, is the result of only *one* distillation, its unique character stamped on it by all those variable factors, in their most extreme form. It is ferociously expensive, even if you can get hold of it – which, on the whole, you can't. But don't let this put you off; if you're looking for a sure-fire way of winning your spurs as a whisky advocate, this is it:

The Ultimate Bluff

. . . Having first assured total privacy, take an empty whisky bottle from which you have removed the label (make sure the glass isn't embossed with the trade mark of whatever it contained previously) and fill to about two-thirds (more would be vulgar) with an ordinary malt or, if you haven't been able to raise a mortgage to buy one, one of the paler (hence more interesting-looking) **blends** – *J&B Rare* or *Cutty Sark* will do. Invite your guest to sit down while you produce the bottle and pace the room – *premier cru* bluffing, like porridge eating, is best done this way – as you prepare your prey with a long story about how you have an understanding with the distillery (choose one of the obscure ones, just in case) that ensures your supply is distilled only from barley grown by the Findhorn Community, kilned with peat laid down during the Early Bronze Age and cut from a croft adjoining a raised beach, then steeped in water drawn immediately after a light Spring shower with a West-South-Westerly breeze; fermented with one particular yeast, used

previously for the brewing of Fowler's Wee Heavy* and
vaporized in the pot-still dented by Alasdair 'Thumbs'
MacFadyen during the Disruption of 1843; matured in
oak casks which formerly stored a Golden Oloroso made
only by Jesuit Fathers in the Ximenez region of Spain,
and hand-bottled (hence the lack of anything so
commercial as a label) by the seventh son of a seventh
son of one of the MacCrimmons of Skye . . .

Or something like that.

Then pour two drams and, pausing only for some such
appropriately ethnic valediction as *Sliànte mhath,
sliànte mhor*** take it off. To ensure success, instruct
your victim to do so in one go, pressing the spirit against
the hard palate with the tongue before letting it slide
down the gullible gullet. We guarantee this cannot fail;
it renders the bluffee in no fit state to argue the matter.
Whether he or she actually *enjoys* it is, of course,
entirely irrelevant.

If, on the other hand, you actually *do* have your own
supply of single-cask malt we can only presume that you
didn't obtain it by being the sort of person who got where
you are today by sharing the finer things of life with
your fellows. Take it to your corporate-hospitality box
at Covent Garden and drink it all by yourself. And we
hope it chokes you.

---

* A lethally drinkable brew sold, in the interests of public order, in
nip bottles.

** Pronounced Slarngy var, slarngy vor – *Good health, great health!*

Regions

There are 8½ distinct Scottish malt whisky regions, each producing whisky with its own distinctive sort of characteristic bluffery, *viz*:

1. Eastern

Occupying the seaboard of Aberdeenshire.

Characteristics: Bracing, keen, windswept, littoral.

Typical malts: *Glen Garioch*. Waste heat from this distillery is used to grow hothouse tomatoes.

Recommended malts: *Lochnagar*, enjoyed by the Old Man Of (© HRH the Prince of Wales); *Fettercairn*, light and fragrant, ideal for elevenses and much better for you than coffee; *Glenturret*, a Gold Medal winner, but 90 per cent goes for blending so it's difficult to procure.

2. Northern

i.e. north of Fort William but mostly north of Inverness.

Characteristics: Stern, muscular, uncompromising, hyperborean.

Typical malts: *Glenmorangie*, one of the Big names, light, smooth and refreshing (NB: accent on the third syllable, even if it does sound odd); *Tomatin*, a peaty malt that uses water drawn from a tributary of the River Findhorn.

Recommended malts: *Old Pulteney*, a Caithness malt said to have 'some of the strong characteristics of the northern temperament', but it might be a good idea not to say which characteristics these are; *Royal Brackla*, situated in Cawdor (where MacBeth got his first big break) and very hard to obtain; *Balblair*, a distillery dating back to 1790 (or possibly 1749) and famous for its light, crumbly peat – so be sure to describe it as 'light-bodied and aromatic.'

3. Perthshire

A region which, for bluffing purposes, includes Loch Lomond.

Characteristics: Smooth, soft, comfortable, Georgic, effete.

Typical malts: None, really, unless you count *Loch Lomond*, which is what made Snowy squiffy in *Tintin and the Black Island*.

Recommended malts: Pretty well all of them. Insist this region is 'undervalued' – a useful phrase, since it leaves open the question of whether or not it deserves to be. *Glengoyne* can be described as 'a pleasant, unassuming little dram'; the distillery is very pretty, and gets its water from a waterfall.

4. Islands

Not including Islay which is one, but including Oban, which isn't.

Characteristics: Oceanic, temperamental, stoical, insular, or if you've had a few 'ultimately thulian.'

Typical malts: *Highland Park*, an Orkney whisky (the most northerly in Britain); be sure to detect the burning of heather along with the seaweedy peat. The distillery was founded by Magnus Eunson, an illicit distiller who covered up his activities by being a Kirk elder and hiding barrels under the pulpit. It was built, somewhat foolishly, on a hill, so water has to be pumped up to it . . . it's knowing this sort of thing that makes you sound authoritative.

Drinking *Talisker*, the product of Skye's only distillery, may be compared with swallowing a Mahler symphony.

Recommended malts: *Scapa*, Orkney's other whisky: gains in bladder-wrack what it loses in heather; and *Isle of Jura* which 'combines the qualities of Islay malts minus the iodine, and West Highland malts minus the lingering sweetness.' Nonsense like this is essential to the really effective whisky bluff.

5. Lowland

Characteristics: Unassuming, disingenuous, unpretentious, self-effacing.

Most Lowland malts are used for blending; enough said, maybe, except for *Littlemill* which is more than good enough to stand on its own. *Auchentoshan* is a Lowland malt made from Highland water, and the only one to be distilled three times; comment on its smoothness and 'Hibernian undertones.'

6. Islay

Characteristics: Penetrating, mordant, heroic, brackish.

Typical malts: *Laphroaig* (pronounced 'lafroyg'), best described as 'an acquired taste' and definitely a Big Whisky, the sort that lets you know you've had one. Tends to be monopolised by the plus-fours-brigade and suffers from over-reverential hype to the extent that it's in danger of becoming ascetic. *Lagavulin* is made next door to Laphroaig, a situation neither cherishes. It's a less heroic whisky, but arguably more user-friendly. *Bowmore*, a stable-mate of Glen Garioch, kindly donates its waste heat to warm the water in the local swimming pool; *Bruichladdich* (pronounced 'brooich-laddie') is Scotland's most westerly distillery and produces a warm, golden whisky that is astonishingly easy to drink.

Recommended malts: *Ardbeg*, closed during much of the eighties owing to one of Britain's periodic outbreaks of economic recovery, but now back in business: be the first to claim to have sampled *Ardbeg nouveau* round about 1997; *Bunnahabhainn* ('boon-a-harven') has a much less peaty-seaweedy flavour than most Islay malts, and a good deal of it ends up in *Famous Grouse*; *Caol Ila* ('cole-eeler') is probably the most mentionable, being almost unheard-of and hard to get (unless you live in Italy or Venezuela); it has a singed-wickerwork flavour, which you can ascribe to the original moisture of the malted barley being 2 per cent rather than the usual 3 per cent. This has probably got nothing to do with it, but that's beside the point.

7. Campbeltown

Only two left; there used to be 20-odd; a situation you deplore.

Characteristics: Inimitable, enigmatic, ineffable.

Recommended malts: Both of them: *Glen Scotia* can be described as 'robust' and praised (or blamed) for its **guff** (see **Glossary**); the distillery is haunted by the shade of its nineteenth century owner, who drowned himself after being tricked out of his savings on a sea cruise. *Springbank* is one of the few private operations still in the hands of the family who founded it (in 1828) and one of only two (the other is *Glenfiddich*) where everything, including bottling, is done on the premises: this ought to predispose sentimentalists to approve the product.

8. Speyside

Dozens of these, mostly clustered about a line from Elgin to Dufftown. Be sure to quote the old Speyside jingle: *Rome was built on seven hills; Dufftown stands on seven stills*. The fame of all Speyside whiskies rests on the water, but hardly any distilleries actually draw theirs from the Spey itself. This is what experts call a 'phenomenological oxymoron', and the rest of us call a flat contradiction.

Characteristics: Pure, scarifying, ethereal, spiritual, rounded, Grampian.

Typical malts: Two of the Big Whiskies are here, *Glenfiddich* and *The Macallan*. There's not much bluffing to be done with these except to say that, on the whole, they deserve their reputation; this sounds as though you've done a lot of comparative research and are not the sort to be taken in by general opinion. Suggest that *Cardhu* and *Linkwood* deserve to be much better known.

Recommended malts: All the ones of which little is heard, e.g. *Convalmore* (available once in a blue moon, at 16 and 18 years old), *Glendullan* (supposedly the favourite tipple of Edward VII), *Glenallachie* (export only), *Knockando* (pron. 'croch-an-doo'), the only whisky to give the dates of both distilling and bottling on the label, so you can sound excessively knowledgable if you decant it first, and *Mortlach* (full-bodied but light on the peat, and a fanatic's favourite).

The town of **Elgin** in this region is bluffing material on two counts:

a) It is the home of *Linkwood*, whose one-time manager (a Mr Roderick MacKenzie) forbade the removal of spiders' webs from the stillroom in the belief that they contributed to the quality of the product;

b) It is the home of **Gordon & MacPhail**, whose shop in South Street is a Mecca for fundamentalists. As well as stocking dozens of otherwise barely-obtainable single malts under their 'Connoisseur's Choice' label, they also have a sample of *Mortlach* dating from the brief reign of Edward VIII and some 25-year-old *Glenlivet* distilled during the Battle of Britain. On no account should you attempt to bluff your way in this hallowed sanctum; even venturing a mild opinion is only recommended for the brave. It might be wiser just to pretend you've been there.

8½. Glenlivet

Characteristics: Unmistakable.

Glenlivet is an essential but dangerous bluffing zone: essential, because it's where most of the best malts come from (or claim to come from), dangerous because it tends to be inhabited by the most ferocious sort of dedicated whisky drinker, who might just know more than you're pretending to. This won't do, and the only proof against it is a crash course in:

Glenlivetology

All you really need to know is that Glenlivet is in Speyside (top of the sticking-out bit on the right-hand side of Scotland), location of 57 malt whisky distilleries for reasons that are mostly to do with **water** and history. To this valley came a refugee from the lost Jacobite cause; his name was Gow – which is from the Gaelic word for a smith – so, in order to outwit the pursuing Hanoverians, he cleverly changed his name to Smith. Smith (whose first name was J) set up a distillery and passed it on to his son and grandson, who carried on making Glenlivet whisky in the traditional way, i.e. without paying tax. George IV, on a visit to Scotland in 1822, claimed he drank nothing else but illegal Glenlivet. This made things even more Romantic, not to mention profitable. The grandson (G) then bought himself a licence from the government so as to make whisky without all the excitement of dawn raids, midnight keg-laden flits through the heather hotly pursued by redcoats, and so on. Two other distillers soon followed his example. Their former colleagues took a dim view of this and threatened to burn down the three distilleries with their coat-turning occupants inside them. Smith is reported to have 'slept with two hair-trigger pistols under his pillow.'

By the mid-nineteenth century, G. Smith and his son (J.G.) had built a new, much bigger distillery and the Glenlivet name had become highly popular – so popular, in fact, that dozens of other distilleries (some of them fifty miles away) were using it. J.G. Smith went to court in 1871 and won (or, as some say, lost) a famous judgement, viz:

- That only his whisky could call itself The Glenlivet;

- That the others could hyphenate their names with it.

This was very canny – a thing all Scots are supposed to be, when they're not being Romantic. The firm of G & JG Smith is now a subsidiary of The Glenlivet and Glen Grant Distilleries Ltd., which is a subsidiary of The Glenlivet Distillers Ltd., which is a subsidiary of Seagram plc, one of the world's biggest multinationals. 'This is highly predictable,' you say. 'Still, at least Guinness didn't get their hands on it.'

You have no choice but to acknowledge that *G & JG Smith's Glenlivet* (**The** Glenlivet) is the best malt whisky there is, was, or ever will be; this is because (a) it probably is (was, etc.) and (b) it's got a very lovely label. There can be no limit to your appreciation of the stuff – though this doesn't mean you have to like it. The true bluffer needn't actually drink Glenlivet whisky at all – all he or she has to do is insist that the one required brand, the only one worth crossing the road for, isn't available. Short of inventing one (e.g. Mitsubishi-Glenlivet) we suggest

Pittyvaich-Glenlivet (virtually unobtainable) or *Glen Keith-Glenlivet* (totally unobtainable because it all goes into a blend called *Natu Nobilis* which you can only get in North America). There are seventeen hyphenated Glenlivets altogether and so long as you steer clear of **Elgin** you're unlikely to find them all in one place.

Alternatively, you could point out that within a circle drawn to include all the distilleries which claim 'Glenlivet' in their name there are thirty-odd distilleries that don't, although they'd have as much right to as the ones who do. You may compare this with the Burgundy/Beaujolais debate. Among these unhyphenated malt whiskies is *The Macallan*, which shares with *Glenfiddich* the distinction of being a malt whisky most people have actually heard of. Observe that *The Macallan* is distilled by a company called Macallan-Glenlivet and indeed was, once upon a time, known as such; presumably they thought the word 'The' sounded classier. This sort of high-altitude snobbery is meat and drink to true believers.

Other well-known quasi-Glenlivets are *Aberlour, Dufftown, Glenfarclas, Glen Grant,* and *Tamdhu*. For bluffing purposes, however, we recommend a quasi-Glenlivet non-Glenlivet, and the best of these is a malt called *Dallas Mhor*; a good choice because it's:

a) distilled in the Glenlivet area (give or take a bit);
b) a rather odd name;
c) pretty well unheard of, and
d) not made any more.*

---

* Unavailable whisky is a good bluffer's ploy, as in 'of course, if you really want to taste a good whisky . . .'

Nearly all blends, however inexpensive, contain trace elements of *The Glenlivet* and however down-market you go the chances are you'll find a smidgen of some sort of Glenlivet, somewhere. Claim to be able to recognise its 'unique Speyside character-istics'. If challenged to describe what these are, say: 'Oh, quite different from those of any other region. Absolutely distinctive. Granitic. Thoroughly Gram-pian.' This sort of appreciative gobbledegook usually goes down a treat with professional whisky drinkers. It seems to mean something to them. Perhaps, secretly, they all have to buy the cut-price kind, too.

All malt whiskies must, of course, at all times be referred to as *distinctive*.

BLENDED WHISKY

Blended whisky is the stuff that most people think of as being 'whisky' or 'Scotch' (the word that must never be used). Blended whisky is a mixture of malt whisky and grain whisky.

The practice of blending took off in the second half of the nineteenth century; up till then the words 'whisky' and 'malt' were interchangeable. The first marketed blend was launched in 1853. Called *Usher's Old Vatted Glenlivet*, it was remarkable for being neither old nor, for the most part, Glenlivet. Much has changed since then, and the practice of blending is now a highly skilled and tightly regulated business.

Nowadays most malt whisky production goes for blending, and blends are mostly four years old, though one or two (e.g. *Mackinlays*) are five. The most affordable ones have been matured for the legal minimum of three.

All blended Scotch whiskies, then, contain a proportion of the Real Stuff. The question is how much, and which? Luckily this is a question which, for 99 per cent of all available blends, cannot be answered. Be sure to take full advantage of this mystery.

What's in it?

You'd be better advised to try cracking the formula of Lea & Perrin's Worcestershire sauce, than attempt to discover what has gone into a bottle of your usual brand of blended whisky. Though quite why the manufacturers should wish their formulae to remain secret from each other, and from the drinker, is, you may suggest, "a riddle wrapped in a mystery inside an enigma" (courtesy of Winston Churchill, a brandy man but a good friend to whisky nonetheless. In 1945 he ensured that supplies of barley went to the distillers instead of being frittered away on such post-war luxuries as food).

Producers of blended whisky will tell you that their fine produce is the result of exhaustive testing of as many as fifty different sorts of malt and grain spirit, and that they dare not, for fear of precipitating the Apocalypse, reveal its mysteries.

They will say that their blenders '**nose**' the various constituents (such a waste of a perfectly good mouth) a process which has been continued man-and-boy down umpteen generations of trusty, rhinocentric perfectionists. It enables them to tell the difference after one sniff, between a blend of character and distinction, and the rest. Then they have to endure seeing the produce of their perfected skills being passed on to the advertisers who depict it defiled with ice or fizzy mixers. This must be very depressing for them.

Meanwhile all the bluffer needs to remember is that:

1. The average blended brand will contain 20-39 per cent malt whisky, the dearer ones 40-50 per cent, and many economy blends as little as 10 per cent.

2. Two blended whiskies which do declare themselves, and which you of course, will keep very quiet about about are:

   Old Highland Blend (Eldridge, Pope & Co., Dorset). Principal malts are *Glenfarclas, Glenfiddich, Glen Grant* and *Glenrothes-Glenlivet*.

39

Queen's Liqueur (W.G. McFadden & Co., Giffnock).
50 per cent malt whisky, *viz: Glen Grant* and *The
Glenlivet*.

The serious bluffer will always have a decanter of one of
these handy.

Secrecy, then, gives you plenty of room for man-
oeuvre. One straightforward bluff is to name

(a) your favourite malt
(b) your preferred blend

and insist that (b) contains a significant amount of (a).
Unless the person you're talking to happens to be the
distiller of (a) or the blender of (b) there's no way of
being caught out.

One of the few popular blends you can be really sure
about is *White Horse* which, you will observe, contains a
significant amount of *Lagavulin*. You will claim to be
able to tell this from the creamy, peaty smoothness –
round, with just a sharp hint of bladder-wrack – which
is the unmistakable characteristic of this Islay single
malt. The fact that the main entrance to Lagavulin
has a big picture of a graminiverous quadruped and a
sign saying WELCOME TO THE WHITE HORSE
DISTILLERY is, of course, entirely immaterial.

Similarly, your detection of *Laphroaig* and *Tormore*
in *Long John* will have nothing to do with the fact that
the former are owned by the latter, while the presence
of *Bunnahabhainn* and *Highland Park* in *Famous
Grouse* is a matter of taste and experience rather than
knowledge that all three are part of the Highland
Distilleries Group.

When in doubt, it is safe to assume a connection
between the malts and blends of the Distillers Group:
this gives you plenty (some would say, more than

enough) to choose from. Or, to put it another way: 'Don't be vague, ask for ... a big dollop of grain whisky containing trace elements of *Aberfeldy, Auchmore, Balmenach, Benmore, Bladnoch, Caol Ila, Cardhu, Clynelish, Dallas Dhu, Dalwhinnie, Glen Albyn, Glendullan ...*' to name but a few. Note, however, that *Haig* isn't in the Distillers Group any more. They had to sell it to pay for the costs of being taken over by Guinness.

De luxe or Premium blends

Generally, a de luxe blend ought to justify its higher price by having more malt in it (at least 50 per cent) and being older (8 years old or more) than the standard fare. Pot-distilling takes longer and maize is about half the price of barley, so the higher price of de luxe whisky can be justified if there's appreciably more malt in the blend. But it can be quite a big 'if'.

All maturer, maltier blends will be more expensive, but not all the more expensive blends are necessarily maturer or maltier. And blenders who give this information away are rarer than hen's teeth. Bell's *Islander* contains Islay malts (as its name implies); otherwise, you're pretty well on your own.

An excellent point to make is that not all malt whiskies blend well together; a de luxe blend may contain (say) 60 per cent malt whiskies and have been aged for ten years but this doesn't mean it will be good to drink if the malts used are not the sort that 'marry' well: thus one can always dismiss someone else's de luxe blend as 'a *disastrous misalliance*'. A really awful one might be positively non-consanguinous, or even morganatic. This is a good ploy for those who would rather not admit to being hard up.

Alternatively – and especially if bluffing in the

company of socialists, Greens, hunt saboteurs and the like – point out that one of the better-known blends, *Islay Mist*, was originally concocted in honour of the coming-of-age of the man who went on to become President of the British Field Sports Association and Britain's last created hereditary baron. This could be a pretty good reason for letting someone else buy it.

Super De luxe blends

Around 20 years old, around 75 per cent malt, and not much change out of a £50 note. 'You could buy two bottles of a first-class unadulterated malt for the price of a bottle of this,' you observe, as you hold out your glass for a refill. 'Still, just to keep you company…'

Supermarket blends

What few of us will admit to drinking: likely to be three years old (just) and no more than 15 per cent malt. However, since most of us do buy it, we recommend it be decanted and passed off as having been blended 'to your taste' by one of your contacts north of the Highland Line (a mythical but useful barrier in this case). *De gustibus non est disputandum*, as they say in Drumnadrochit.

Choose supermarket 'own-brand' in preference to cheaper labels with names like 'Hoots Mon!' or 'Big Yin': supermarket chains have a reputation to defend. Read the label carefully and, if it says '37.5 alcohol/65° proof', put the bottle back on the shelf with a curl of the lip and a barely suppressed hiss. Under-proofing may be fine for gin (you just drink more gin or add less tonic) but drinking under-proof whisky is only for the truly desperate, i.e. when there's nothing else left on the shelf.

Miniatures

Many tourists will, when deprived of any other sort of item, buy miniature bottles of whisky, some of which are brands that have no existence in any other sort of container. Bluffers should have no truck with them, except when they're offered free by distillery managers. Point out that collecting miniature whiskies is a singularly senseless hobby, since they're worthless if you open them, and pointless if you don't. Their cost prices the contents at around a pound a sip, which is absurd by any standards.

You may, however, evince a passing fondness for the following miniatures of Scotch whisky, bourbon and Canadian rye: *Old Taylor, Old Forester, Cairngorm, Four Roses, Dimple Haig, Hiram Walker, Harper's, Kentucky Tavern, Red Label, Dunosdale Cream, Lord Calvert, George IV, Queen Anne, Highland Queen, Vat 69, Standfast* and *Old Argyll*. These were all the pieces drunk during the famous game of draughts between Wormold and Captain Segura in *Our Man in Havana*.

Name Your Bluff

Malt whiskies tend to take their brand names from their distilleries; most blended whiskies, on the other hand, appear to have been christened by the sort of people who go on to call their retirement bungalows 'Erzanmine'.

Common names

In their unrelenting quest for a name that sounds vaguely Scottish and Romantic, blenders often seem to have got stuck in a misty Caledonian groove, e.g.

Black First name of twenty-two whiskies, presumably inspired by the Black Watch, the black grouse, Black Donald of the Isles, the Black Knight of Lorne, the Black Acts, blackface sheep, etc. Known in trendy left-wing circles as 'without-milk'. *Black & White* whisky is enjoyed by British Members of Parliament under a House of Commons label.

Bonnie First name of half a dozen deservedly unheard-of brands which, you will maintain, are drunk only by people who display nodding Loch Ness Monsters in their rear car windows.

Clan First name of fourteen whiskies, including *Clan Campbell* (owned by Pernod), *Clan House* (The Rum Co. Ltd. of Basle), and *Clan Munro* (the General Beverage Corp. of Luxembourg, better known as Martini-Rossi).

Glen First name/prefix of 127 whiskies, not counting strength or age variations of the same brand. There's even one called *Glenmillar*. Claim to be on a lifetime's quest to track down and sample all 127 including *Glenkinchie,* the last single malt in the Lothians. It's extraordinary how eager people can be to help with this sort of ludicrous project.

Gold/Golden First name of 27 whiskies, six of them called Gold Label. *Fleischsmann's Golden Glen* is the highly improbable name of a blended whisky shipped from Scotland in bulk and bottled in the United States.

Highland First name of 39 whiskies. *Highland Queen* (named after the one who lost her head) was the first whisky ever to be marketed in Egypt, and is rumoured to contain more malt than most.

King/King's First name of 44 whiskies including *King Dick* (no comment), *King Size*, *King Alfred* (cakes added to the peat) and the probably blasphemous *King of Kings*. Most of Scotland's kings were called Robert, James or Alexander, but there isn't a whisky named after Alexander and *MacBeth* is no longer available. Some rather unlikely English monarchs are, however, represented by the splendid firm of Henry Stenham & Co., whose blends include: *King Edgar, King Edmund II, King John, King Henry VIII* and *Old Arthur*. Stenham's offers all its 35 whiskies in a choice of ages (3, 5, 8, 10 and 12 years old) and bottle shapes, which is good fun.

Old First name of 85 whiskies (101 if you count 'Auld') some of which are very silly (see **Silly names**). Look out for *Old Fettercairn* single malt: it's distilled by a firm founded by Mr Gladstone's father, which probably explains W.E.G's. knowledge of the angel's share and sympathy for the respectable drinking classes.

Queen/Queen's First name of 21 whiskies, including *Queen's Liqueur* and two *Queen Elizabeths*.

Royal First name of 62 whiskies, most of which are exported to republics. None of them is by appointment to HM the Queen.

Watch out for the frequent use of **rare** and **special** in brand names. Their meaning can be defined as

   (a) expensive
   (b) ordinary
or (c) both.

Silly names

There is no need to invent your own when you can choose from the following real ones:

Blue Hanger, Gee Gee, Glen Tosh, Grog Blossom, Kilt Castle, Mac King Gay Ghost, Monster's Choice, Old Age, Old Barrister, Old Cobblers, Old Crypt, Old Fellah, Old Label, Pheasant Plucker, Pig's Nose, Plus Fours, Queen Size, Red Capsule, Red Tape, Regal Butt, Royal Pheasant, Scotch Pillar, Sheep Dip, Tee Tee, Twinkle, Upstairs, Wat Tyler and *Wham's Dram.*

Suggest the silliest ones of all are derived from the names of fishing flies.

Phoney names

Foreign brands of so-called **'Scotch whisky'** can be made by mixing small quantites of exported malt with large quantities of home-made heaven-knows-what and selling them under authentic-sounding names, e.g. *Captain Jock* (Greece) and *Loch Ness Scotch Whisky* (Italy)*, both of which have been suppressed following legal action.

All good bluffers should claim to have sampled some of the following currently available overseas:

Duck Scot (Brazil)
Gaylord (Germany)
Old Windjammer (Italy)
Camerone Cream of the Glen (Malawi)
Kilt (Spain)
King Victoria (Japan)
Auld Piss (Ecuador).

---

* **Italy** is easily the world's biggest importer of bottled malt whisky. No-one knows why.

Naughty names

A good parlour game is to dream up names of whiskies NOT marketed by the Distillers Group/Guinness plc. Try the following for starters: *Queen's Counsel, Sub Judice, Auld Arbitrageur, Saunders' Special Reserve, Numbered Account, Glenzurich, Backhander, Scots Headquarters, Services Rendered, Dementia Præcox* and *Knight's Farewell*.

'Scotch' – a warning

Scotch Whisky is defined in European Community legislation as (among other things) 'Whisky which has been distilled in Scotland'. This gives due recognition to the unique qualities of Scottish water, air, peat, climate, industrial relations and so forth.

There are two things to avoid, however, *viz:*

1. Calling Scotch whisky 'Scotch', which is considered vulgar.

2. Calling malt whisky 'Scotch whisky', which is not merely vulgar but also wrong, since the law allows Scotch whisky to be distilled from various inferior cereals as well as malted barley.

Refer any disbeliever to the report of the 1908 Royal Commission – 'Whisky is a spirit obtained by distillation from a mash of cereal grains saccharified by the diastase of malt' – and point out that only the peculiar genius of the great and the good could make such a nobly enjoyable thing as whisky sound so horribly unattractive.

Amaze your audience by remarking that the value of whisky currently maturing in casks in Scotland far exceeds that of all the Bank of England's gold reserves.

'It makes you think,' you murmur. Then quote Rabelais, and hold your glass out.

Labels

Labels, especially those on blended whiskies, give very little away and should be admired for their artistry rather than read for their information. Remember that only whisky distilled (and, preferably, blended though not necessarily bottled) in Scotland is allowed to call itself 'Scotch whisky' and that anything purporting to be a single malt should state the name of the distillery whence it came; any malt that doesn't is probably a **vatted** one. Look for the capacity (75cl on an ordinary bottle) and alcoholic strength (at least 70° or 40 per cent by volume).

Note that words like *Special, Finest, Extra, Old/Auld, Reserve, Supreme, Cream, Ancient, Matured* etc. are, though quite possibly reassuring (like the old claim of Carnation milk to come from contented cows), completely meaningless. First prize for appealing labelling probably ought to go to Hedges & Butler, specialists in the aristocratic end of the blended market, whose brands are (in ascending order of pomp and ceremony): *Royal, Royal Special De Luxe, Royal Finest De Luxe, Royal Supreme De Luxe* and *Royal Imperial De Luxe*. This rather suggests that 'finest' and 'supreme' aren't intended to be taken too seriously; 'special' by this token means 'relatively ordinary.'

A close runner-up is Dewar's, whose posh blend goes under the name of *Dewar's De Luxe Ancestor*; people with ordinary, run-of-the-mill pedigrees probably ought to leave it alone. You can safely describe *Dewar's Ne Plus Ultra* as 'unique' without bothering to taste it.

Note that the ordinary blend is known as 'White Label' in the UK and 'Dooers' in the US.

You should insist that *Vat 69* has never tasted the same since they stopped putting a wax seal on the bottle, and observe that it got its name as a result of a blind tasting session of a number of vats of experimental blended whiskies. Or so the story goes; you could speculate aloud as to what sort of state the tasters' palates were in after sampling the other 68.

Famous Grouse is known simply as 'Grouse' among the cognoscenti, who naturally despise anyone foolish enough to be taken in by a self-fulfilling marketing ploy like the use of the word 'famous' on a label. It is popular among experts for its superior malty flavour despite the higher-than-average price, and popular with ordinary mortals for exactly the opposite reason.

Be somewhat contemptuous of anyone who buys one of the brands sold only in pseudo-authentic stone flagons; *Usquebach* is one such, a toe-curling misspelling of the Gaelic. Another is *Ye Whisky of Ye Monks*, a de luxe blend that sounds as though it ought to be distilled, blended and bottled in a theme park.

For dedicated label-bluffers we recommend two blends in particular:

Te Bheag nan Eilean (pronounced 'tchay vek nan yellan') – the sole blend of a company based on the tiny Isle Ornsay (or *Eilean Iarmain*) off the south coast of Skye and run by a reformed merchant banker with a passion for Gaelic and fancy whisky labels. It contains a pleasingly high proportion of 5-12 year old Speyside malts, so be sure to taste, name and date a few of them. No-one will be able to prove you wrong.

Uam Var – a blended whisky produced by the makers of Drambuie.

The only really safe ploy – since you can pretty well make it up as you go along with the help of as many **bluffing elements** as you can muster all at one go – is to declare that you're only interested in the quality and provenance of the contents, rather than such artifices as baroque labels, ribbons, blobs of wax, or dangly gold bells round the neck of the bottle.

Single Grain

Rarely available – *Cameron Brig* and *The Invergordon* are two you can mention – single grain whiskies are 100 per cent silent spirit, i.e. the product of a patent still and containing *no malt whisky at all*. Amazing but true: absolutely none whatsoever. You should describe its flavour as *distinctive* (naturally) while noting that the professionals all agree on its 'rather peculiar medicinal flavour', although they don't actually say which peculiar medicine they have in mind.

Whisky Notes

Mixers

Mixers ought generally to be deprecated outside the privacy of your own drinks cupboard; reserve your most withering scorn for soda, but note in passing that some of the nastiest concoctions (e.g. whisky-and-Lucozade) were invented in the West Highlands. There are only two mixers you should allow:

- Water, from a Highland tap or an expensive bottle;
- More whisky.

Glass

Whisky should be drunk from a cylindrical glass, preferably cut crystal with a design that reaches at least one-third of the way up (so you know how much whisky to put in) and a heavy bottom (to make that satisfying clunk when you put it down). Avoid the hip flask unless you fill it with economy blend; your body heat, and the reaction of the spirit with the metal, will then obscure the rebarbative flavour. Anyone who serves you malt whisky in a brandy balloon is a terminal poser, more deserving of pity than contempt.

Hangover

Drinkers of good whisky (though not always good whisky drinkers) never have hangovers. The dry throat and pounding head syndrome is, therefore, entirely the result of *involuntary poisoning*, caused by (for example) an excess of fusel oils, an imbalance in the malt-grain ratio, an allergy to caramel, a systemic intolerance to certain barley, etc., *never* by over-indulgence.

GLOSSARY – The Process

The making of malt whisky employs a sumptuous vocabulary, something like a cross between a sex manual and a handbook of Masonic ritual. Short of wading through various worthy tomes on the subject (a thing no self-respecting bluffer would ever do) your only other hope of becoming fluent in whiskybabble is to join a conducted tour of a distillery. This has one big advantage – you get a free dram at the end of it (not at the beginning – too many people would escape) and two big disadvantages:

1. If the distillery is in operation you can't hear what's being explained to you and the staff all have better things to do, e.g. malting, grinding, sparging, mashing, brewing, stilling, rummaging, not to mention *waiting for the foreshot*;

2. If the distillery is not in operation because you're visiting during the **silent season** (July-Sept) you can hear all right but you might as well have stayed at home because there's nothing to look at, and the staff are all busy gardening.

Either way it's a bit too much like hard work. Much better to pour yourself a fat dram, put your feet up, and let us take the tour for you, thus:

Rough dressing – The removal from barley of odd bits of stalk, fieldmouse and combine harvester that might have sneaked in.

Malting – Germination of damp barley to turn it into malt; regularly raked and turned to prevent its sproutlets becoming entangled.

Kilning – Part-roasting of germinated barley grains over a peat furnace in line with the Highland Heritage (Marketing) Act, the Euro-Peat Directive (number 2746/xviii/D) and the Scottish Tourist Board's Ethnic Aroma Initiative.

Grist – The little-known origin of the well-known expression, 'grist to the mill' and what whole grain is ground down into before being used for brewing and distilling, or wasted on luxuries like bread.

Tun room – The first (or, in the US, second) floor of a distillery, containing a number of huge vessels whose bottoms are located on the floor below.

Sparging – Exciting word for the otherwise fairly tedious business of pouring very hot (but not boiling) water over malt grist.

Mash tun – Sort of brobdingnagian Ascot boiler used for sparging and...

Mashing – What goes on in the mash tun, after sparging; think of 'mash' as in tea, rather than potatoes.

Balfour-Schock-Gusmer Lauteran – Fine old Highland name for a white-hot technological, fifth-generation sort of mash tun which may (or may not) contribute to the unique quality of *Tomatin*.

Extraction waters – Queasily obstetric term for the warm, brown, sticky fluid that is run off from the bottom of the mash tun and then fermented. This happens twice, usually; the third and fourth lots are heated up again – be sure to say 'recycled' – for the next lot of sparging.

Draff – Soggy leftovers of malted barley grist after extraction of the above. Used as cattle-feed.

Worts – What extraction waters turn into during their journey from the mash tun to the...

Wash back – Gargantuan wooden vessel used for fermenting the sugary worts by adding shovelfuls of ravenous yeast and standing well clear.

Wash – What worts turn into after fermentation: a thin, dreary, grizzling sort of sour ale, not entirely unlike low alcohol lager.

Alcohols – Always plural, note: wash contains a large number of *higher* and *lower alcohols*, including ethanol. Remember that it's always better to be thought of as an ethanolophile than spoken of as an alcoholic.

Carbon dioxide – The other product of fermentation. Note that the Loch Lomond distillery captures it, compresses it, and sells it to be turned into the various sorts of fizzy stuff you're not allowed to put in malt whisky.

Stillroom – Situated on the ground (or, in the US, first) floor. Alchemical laboratory; destination of the wash; inhabited by **stillmen**, the aristocracy of the distillery workforce (dent-maintenance operatives, foreshot-watchers, fusel-detectors, men in white coats with Parker pens in their top pockets, etc).

Pot-still – Nuptial chamber of the Chymical Wedding; atavistic union of ying and yang, animus and anima; the large copper retort for the heating, separation, evaporation and re-condensation of various alcohols present in lightly fermented malty water.

Worm – Apt name for the long, thin, coiled-up wiggly tube that comes out of the top of a still and is used for re-condensing evaporated alcohols; you can't see it because it's hidden in a large tank of cold water.

Low wines – Product of the first distillation and quite undrinkable, even with the addition of 7-Up and a couple of cocktail umbrellas.

Pot ale – Leftovers of the first distillation; fed to cattle who no longer get a decent buzz from draff.

Spent lees – Residue of the second distillation, and practically the only by-product that is poured down the drain; being terribly organic, it's obviously very good for something-or-other. Killer algæ, probably.

Spirit still – The end of the line; destination of the low wines.

Spirit safe – Ornately padlocked fishtank through which pass the various end products of the spirit still, *viz*:

Foreshot – Name for all the volatile, flighty alcohols that aren't wanted in whisky. Modern distilleries test for it with state-of-the-art technology (e.g. the Sykes hydrometer, invented in 1818). You should claim to know of one where they still use the much more romantic method of watching it turn a glass of water milky-blue.

Middle cut – This is *it*, the liquid that will be whisky one day. It accounts for approximately 40 per cent of the total output of the spirit still; exactly how much varies from one distillery to another and is, of course, a secret.

Feints – The last lot of alcohols to come off, saved, and added to the next lot of low wines to be distilled. Also known as **aftershot**; use whichever word appeals to you more, acording to the company you're in and the circumstances under which you're in it.

Fusel oil – A heavy alcohol present in the feints, some of which is required in the middle cut in order to give the whisky flavour; it is an essential constituent of **cling** and a contributor to **guff** (see **Glossary 2**) and can be held responsible for any ill effects.

White spirit – Not the stuff with which you clean paintbrushes but freshly-distilled, 120° proof liquor unsullied by water and unadulterated by charcoal, pajarette, caramel, etc. One whiff is usually enough to cauterise the nasal tissue; drinking it may be likened to being hit over the head with a ten-ton bunch of freesias. Claim to like it.

Maturing – a) Process you've gone through in order to become a whisky bluffer; b) Process whisky has gone through in oak casks, usually **butts** (108 gallons) or **hogsheads** (55 gallons), for a minimum of three years in a bonded warehouse.

Cutting – Regrettable practice of diluting white spirit with water before maturing; repeated with mature whisky before bottling.

Proof – a) The action of testing your hypothesis by opening someone else's bottle; b) Fiendishly complicated measurement of alcoholic strength, designed to bamboozle people who aren't fazed by percentages. Originally something to do with the flashpoint of gunpowder: if your gun didn't go off, it meant they were watering the whisky. 100° proof spirit is 57.1% alcohol and 42.9% water. All you need to remember is that 70° proof = 40% alcohol. (In America, where they have smaller gallons and more volatile gunpowder, this re-translates as 80° proof.)

GLOSSARY – The Product

As it is advisable to be familiar with a selection of terms to employ when confronted with the spirit itself, we offer the following, together with their simple definitions.

Appearance

Golden – Anything between brown and yellow.

Citrine – Too pale to be golden.

Fulvous – Too dark to be golden, but 'brown' sounds offensive and only port is allowed to be tawny.

Amber – Yellow.

Clear – You can see right through it. No bits of fruit, cigarette ash, etc.

Pellucid – Use instead of 'clear' when what you can see through the glass is particularly worth looking at.

Lambent – Seems to glow with an inner light.

Limpid – Lambent in a sort of laid-back way.

Incandescent – Looks like you've set fire to it.

Polished – Served in a clean glass.

Serene – Hasn't been served with a fizzy mixer.

Plangent – Cries out to be swallowed.

Rich – You've seen the price on the bottle.

Cling – The snail-trails on the inside of the glass after you've tilted it. An absence of cling means you're about to drink a blended whisky with very little malt in it: prepare to be disparaging. If it was wine one would say it had 'good legs' (which just goes to show what a silly business wine is). Cling is caused by the essential fusel oils in malt whisky, so its presence is highly encouraging.

Nose

Brisk – 'Hang on a minute, I seem to have lost my eyeballs on the ceiling somewhere…'

Ardent – '…not to mention my head.'

Dominant – You've stuck your nose in too far.

Delicate – Doesn't make you squint.

Discreet – Probably isn't whisky.

Insistent – Follows you round the room.

Aromatic – Smells of something other than whisky.

Pungent – Smells of whisky.

Fragrant – Sophisticates' word for 'nice'.

Elusive – You can't think of anything clever to say about it.

Fugitive – The ideal non-committal comment.

Bite – The quality of being just as effective as Vick's vapour rub.

Taste

Insistent – No good sucking a Polo afterwards.

Lingering – No good trying Listerine either.

Haunting – It repeats on you.

Astringent – Makes you worry about your tooth enamel.

Penetrating – You've just lost all your tooth enamel, gums, soft palate...

Assertive – Not awfully nice, frankly.

Peaty – Reminiscent of garden bonfires.

Heathery – Sort of... not quite peaty.

Nutty – Two of these will do instead of lunch.

Pure – Definitely no soda in it.

Littoral – Reminiscent of seaweed, sand, sun oil, etc.

Terrene – Reminiscent of mud.

Sanative – Tastes like medicine.

Mellow – You catch yourself beginning to believe in the United Nations, the tooth fairy, weather forecasts, etc. Nice.

Bracing – You stop believing in the above. Still nice, though.

Light – Suitable for breakfast.

Smooth – Doesn't leave you gasping for air.

Creamy – Clogs the tongue.

Suave – Bland.

Mighty – You happen to know it's something famous, like *Laphroaig*, *The Macallan* or *Smith's Glenlivet*. Most of the above rolled into one.

Distinctive – Definitely some sort of whisky. A word that effortlessly covers an infinite number of *uhmmm* virtues.

Guff – That which makes you go red in the face and start clutching your uvula; 'guff' is pretty close to the noise you make. Blame insufficient maturing and/or too much fusel oil.

Character

A combination of **appearance**, **nose** and **taste** with other factors thrown in, such as history, reputation, bottle shape, design of label, price, etc.

Heroic – Probably a little overrated but you wouldn't fancy picking a quarrel with it.

Noble – Can be used of any whisky that can actually be tasted but which doesn't make you cough, choke, cry, pick arguments with strangers or feel remorseful the following morning; use especially for whiskies you feel deserve to be better-known than they are, like *Clynelish*, *Linkwood*, *Glengarrioch*, *Bruichladdich*, *Talisker*, *King Henry VIII 12-year-old*.

Rounded – Interesting bottle; elegant label; smells fine; tastes nice; doesn't give you heartburn; useful change from £25.

Affected – Any whisky promoted for its snob-value with advertisements of the only-a-few-of-you-can-afford-me variety.

Austere – Sort of whisky that can only be appreciated after a lifetime's devotion. There are, as it happens, better things to do with a lifetime.

Ascetic – Appealing to all the senses except those of taste and smell.

Numinous – After two glasses you decide to teach yourself Gaelic.

Generous – The ultimate accolade; to be used of whiskies which, to quote famous former excise officer turned writer Neil Gunn:

> '...recall the world of hills and glens, of raging elements, of shelter, of divine ease...The essential oils that wind in the glass uncurl their long fingers in lingering benediction, and the nobler works of Creation are made manifest...'

Note that a glass or two of a really generous whisky would enable you to recall bens, glens, etc., even if you'd lived all your life in Snake Pit, Arizona.

Alternatively, apply the term to any whisky served by an open-handed host and, if it brings out the same qualities in you, feel free to call it **noble** as well. And have another one, why not.

THE AUTHOR

In 1978 David Milsted moved from England to Highland Park and Scapa; then he lived for four years in Ardbeg, Lagavulin, Laphroaig, Bowmore, Bruichladdich, Bunnahabhainn and Caol Ila. He now lives in Talisker. A professional author, he would choose to work in a distillery if he ever had to get a proper job.

THE BLUFFER'S GUIDES®